TIME TRAVEL GUIDES

ANCIENT EGYPT

Liz Gogerly

www.raintree.co.uk/library
Visit our website to find out more information about Raintree books.

To order:

Phone 44 (0) 1865 888112

Send a fax to 44 (0) 1865 314091

Visit the Raintree bookshop at www.raintree.co.uk/library to browse our catalogue and order online.

First published in Great Britain by Raintree, Halley Court, Jordan Hill, Oxford OX2 8EJ, part of Harcourt Education. Raintree is a registered trademark of Harcourt Education Ltd.

Editorial: Clare Weaver, Sarah Shannon, Lucy Beevor, and Harriet Milles
Design: Steve Mead, Rob Norridge, and Geoff Ward
Picture Research: Ruth Blair
Illustrations: Eikon Illustration & Tim Slade
Production: Duncan Gilbert
Originated by Modern Age
Printed and bound in China by South China Printing Company Limited

932'.01
A full catalogue record for this book is available from the British Library.

This levelled text is a version of Freestyle: Time Travel Guides: Ancient Egypt.

Acknowledgements
The publishers would like to thank the following for permission to reproduce photographs:
AKG Images pp. 58–59 (Archives CDA; Guillot), 11, 54–55 (Erich Lessing), 6–7 (Herve Champollion), 41 (Suzanne Held); Alamy p. 34 (Gary Cook); Ancient Art & Architecture Collection Ltd. pp. 44–45 (Mary Jelliffe), 25 (Ronald Sheridan), 12 (Y. Shishido), 23, 38, 39, 40, 48–49; Art Archive pp. 36 (Bibliothèque Musée du Louvre/Dagli Orti), 42–43 (British Museum, London/Dagli Orti), 9, 20, 29, 37, 40, 47 (Egyptian Museum, Cairo/Dagli Orti), 13, 14, 18–19, 21, 28, 46, 53 (Dagli Orti), 58–59 (Egyptian Museum, Turin/Dagli Orti), 16 (Khawam Collection, Paris/Dagli Orti), 15, 17, 21, 22, 30, 44 (Musée du Louvre, Paris/Dagli Orti), 51 (Ragab Papyrus Institute, Cairo/Dagli Orti), 32–33; Corbis pp. 26–27 (Frans Lemmens/Zefa), 31 (Jose Fuste Raga).

Cover images of a necklace with winged scarab pectoral from Tutankhamen's treasure, and Cuff bracelet with eye Oudjat from the tomb of Sheshonq II, 930 BC, reproduced with permission of Ancient Art & Architecture Collection Ltd. Cover photograph of the Sphinx reproduced with permission of Getty Images/ Photodisc.

The publishers would like to thank Christina Riggs for her assistance in the preparation of this book.

CONTENTS

Words that appear in the text in bold, **like this**, are explained in the Glossary.

MEDITERRANEAN SEA

N
W   E
S

WESTERN DESERT

Alexandria

NILE DELTA

Giza   **Memphis**
Saqqara

Herakleopolis

SPHINX AND
GREAT PYRAMIDS

NILE RIVER

Abydos

Thebes
   Dahamsha

Hierakonpolis

Philae
   Aswan

TEMPLE OF KARNAK

DEAD SEA

VALLEY OF THE KINGS

MAP OF ANCIENT EGYPT

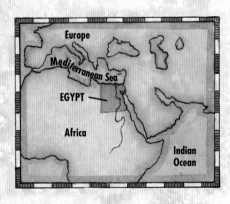

Europe

Mediterranean Sea

EGYPT

Africa

Indian
Ocean

SINAI PENINSULA

The magnificent
pyramids at Giza.
Khufu's Great Pyramid
is the biggest stone
structure in the world.

CHAPTER 1

FACTS ABOUT ANCIENT EGYPT

Ancient Egypt is like no other place on Earth. You will see the pyramids and tombs. The Egyptian kings called **pharaohs** are buried there. You will have a trip of a lifetime.

This section tells you the best times to visit and when not to go. It will tell you information about the weather. You will find out lots more about this exciting country.

WHEN TO TRAVEL

Ancient Egypt has a long and exciting history. It spans more than 3,000 years. Its history is divided into periods (number of years), and then into dynasties.

A dynasty is the time that one family or group of **pharaohs** ruled ancient Egypt.

TIMELINE OF ANCIENT EGYPT

Below is a list of Kings in each period. (Note: dates given are approximate.)

EARLY DYNASTIC PERIOD (3100–2686 BC)

1st Dynasty
   Narmer (3100 BC)

OLD KINGDOM (2686–2181 BC)

4th Dynasty
   Khufu (2589–2566 BC)
   Khafre (2558–2532 BC)

FIRST INTERMEDIATE PERIOD (2181–2055 BC)

MIDDLE KINGDOM (2055–1650 BC)

11th Dynasty
   Mentuhotep II (2055–2004 BC)

SECOND INTERMEDIATE PERIOD (1650–1550 BC)

NEW KINGDOM (1550–1069 BC)

18th Dynasty
   Amenhotep II (1427–1400 BC)
   Ramesses II (1279–1213 BC)

THIRD INTERMEDIATE PERIOD (1069–747 BC)

Key:
   Stay away
   Okay times to visit
   Best times to visit

EARLY TIMES

The Early Dynastic Period is a good time to visit. King Narmer of Upper Egypt has just defeated the ruler of Lower Egypt.

OLD KINGDOM

If you arrive during the Old Kingdom, travel to Memphis. This is the centre of power.

MIDDLE KINGDOM

For a quiet trip, travel during the Middle Kingdom. Mentuhotep II is building a temple near the **capital** city Thebes. A capital is the most important city in a country.

NEW KINGDOM

Egypt is now the most powerful **empire** in the ancient world. An empire is a group of countries ruled by one leader.

WHEN NOT TO TRAVEL

- During the First Intermediate Period. There is fighting and foreign invasion. Foreign means from outside the country. There are also **plagues** (deadly diseases).
- In the Second Intermediate Period. Groups of foreign people have taken control.
- In the Third Intermediate Period and the Late Period. More foreign invasions.

Ramesses II ("The Great") was a strong ruler of the New Kingdom. His time in power would be another good time to visit.

GEOGRAPHY AND CLIMATE

The River Nile flows northwards for over 965 km (600 miles). Then it spreads out to form a **delta**. A delta is made up of many streams. The Nile Delta flows into the Mediterranean Sea.

RED AND BLACK LAND

The strip of land surrounding the Nile is called Kemet, or "Black Land". It is named after the black **silt** that is washed up by the Nile when it floods. Silt is **fertile** mud. This mud is full of good things that help plants grow. The desert beyond is called Deshret, or "Red Land".

THE SEASONS OF THE NILE

The Nile even makes the seasons. From July to October the fields are flooded. The farmers can't work. They find other work instead. Some work as builders. From November to February the farmers are back in the fields. In March to June the farmers harvest or gather in their crops. They grow fruit and vegetables.

Most ancient Egyptians live on the fertile land surrounding the Nile. The river is important for drinking water, fish, and much more.

GOOD NILE OR BAD NILE?

The locals talk about "a good Nile" or "a bad Nile". "A good Nile" means that the Nile has flooded the fields along its banks. There will be a good harvest. If it's "a bad Nile" then perhaps the river didn't flood. There might not be enough water for the crops. People might go hungry.

CUSTOMS AND CULTURE

"GOD-KING"

Most rulers in ancient Egypt are men, called **pharaohs**. Egyptians think the pharaoh has control over everyday things. Ancient Egyptians kiss the ground the pharaoh has walked on!

GOVERNMENT

The pharaoh controls the running of the country. Second to the pharaoh is a kind of prime minister. He is called a **vizier**. There are also other people called officials. They help run the government. The government is made up of people who run the country.

CLASS SYSTEM

The class system puts people into different groups or levels. At the top of the class system are the pharaoh and royal family. Next there are the **aristocracy** (noble people) and other important people.

The pharaohs of ancient Egypt wear a false beard. It helps to make them look intelligent and wise.

Next come **scribes** and rich land owners. Scribes copy books or papers by hand.

The rest of the people are at the bottom. People believe that the gods decide a person's place in society.

WOMEN

Women from important or wealthy families have many rights. For example, they can run businesses.

A scribe uses a reed and ink for writing. A reed is a plant.

Women from the lower classes are treated as second-class citizens. They must obey their husband. Many women stay at home. Some women do work outside the home.

CHILDREN

Families like to have lots of children. Only the boys of wealthy families go to school. Many children have to work.

Girls often marry as young as 12 years old. Boys get married at 14 years old.

RELIGION

Religion is very important to ancient Egyptians. They worship many different gods and goddesses. They believe the gods have power over everything that happens. For example, they believe the gods have power over the weather.

This is the Dendara Zodiac. ↲ It shows many of the gods and goddesses of ancient Egypt.

KEEPING THE BALANCE

Keeping order in the universe is very important to ancient Egyptians. So is keeping balance. They believe the universe is made up of opposites. For example, order and chaos (muddle). People keep order and balance in their lives by being honest and fair.

A GOD FOR EVERYTHING

There are over 2,000 gods in ancient Egypt. The gods can be in human or animal form. They can be a mixture of both. There are national gods. They are worshipped by people all over the country. There are also local gods. They are worshipped by people living in one area.

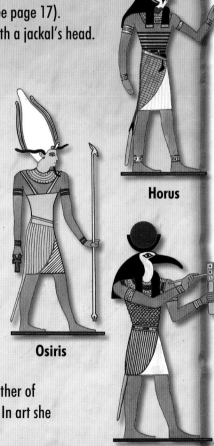

OTHER GODS TO LOOK OUT FOR...

- Anubis — The god of **mummification** (see page 17). In art he is shown as a jackal or a man with a jackal's head.

- Hathor — Goddess of love, children, music, and dance. In pictures she is usually shown as a cow.

- Horus — The ancient god of the sky. The son of Osiris and Isis. Horus is usually shown as a falcon.

- Osiris — Husband and brother of Isis. God of the underworld. Ancient Egyptians believed they passed through the underworld after death. It was full of dangers. Osiris appears in human form.

- Thoth — The god of wisdom and the Moon. On paintings he appears as an ibis (wading bird) or baboon.

- Isis — The greatest goddess of all. The mother of Horus. She has amazing magical powers. In art she appears as a woman.

Horus

Osiris

Thoth

TEMPLES

Temples are not places where you go to worship. Each temple is believed to be the home of a certain god. Temples are run by priests and priestesses.

Ordinary people are not allowed inside temples. However, the buildings are impressive from the outside. They are worth a visit. The most outstanding temples are at Karnak and Luxor (see pages 38–39).

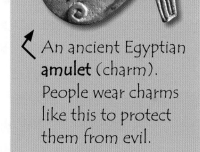

An ancient Egyptian **amulet** (charm). People wear charms like this to protect them from evil.

WAYS OF WORSHIP

The outside walls of some temples are decorated with ears. People whisper into the ears. They are saying their prayers into the ear of the god.

Other people worship by visiting small **shrines**. A shrine is a sacred place. People also leave food, flowers, and gifts at shrines.

ANCIENT MUMMIES

Ancient Egyptians want to live forever. They believe that a dead person's body should be **mummified** (specially preserved). This was done for the **Afterlife**. The Afterlife is where the ancient Egyptians believe the dead go.

Royalty and the top rank are mummified in a special way. Their organs are removed. The corpse (dead body) is dried out. Then it is stuffed. It is covered in oil and perfume. Finally, the corpse is wrapped in linen (cloth) bandages. It is then put in a stone coffin. The coffin is called a **sarcophagus**. The coffin is sealed away in a tomb with food and belongings for the Afterlife.

< A tomb painting of the god of mummification. He is performing a ritual during the burial of a **pharaoh**.

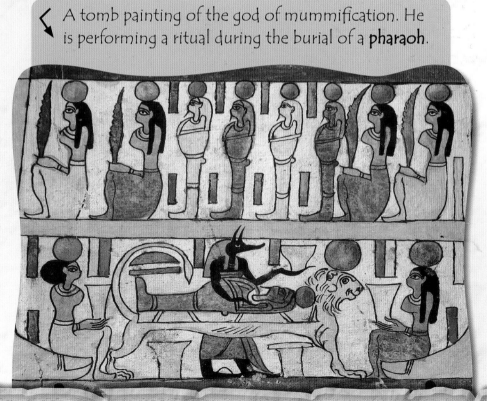

A painted decoration from an 18th Dynasty nobleman's tomb. It shows servants carrying gifts of geese, corn, and fine wine.

CHAPTER 2

USEFUL INFORMATION

Egypt is very hot. You will need cool clothing for your visit. If you don't want to stand out in the crowd then take lots of white clothes. There are delicious fresh fruit and vegetables to eat. The national dish is goose. Everyone drinks beer – even children! The ancient Egyptians don't use money. Read on to find out how you will buy things.

WHAT TO WEAR

The ancient Egyptians have dressed the same way for thousands of years! They have always worn white linen. It feels cool.

All men wear a kind of apron or kilt. They often also wear a kind of tunic-style shirt.

Women wear straight close-fitting dresses. On cool evenings they wear a shawl. Children dress like their parents or they wear nothing at all. Most people do not wear shoes. The rich sometimes wear sandals.

JEWELLERY

Ancient Egyptian jewellery is colourful and eye-catching. People wear jewelled rings, bracelets, earrings, and necklaces. The very rich can afford precious (costly) metals and jewels. The poor make do with pottery beads. Ancient Egyptian jewellery is an ideal gift to take home.

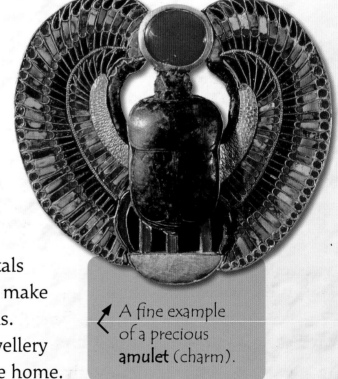

A fine example of a precious **amulet** (charm).

FINISHING TOUCHES

The ancient Egyptians like to look good. Women and men wear make-up. Most people use a black dye as eyeliner. It is called kohl.

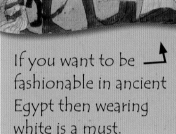

If you want to be fashionable in ancient Egypt then wearing white is a must.

An ancient Egyptian girl with a wig. Beeswax is used to set the style.

Wigs are very popular amongst the upper classes. They help protect them from sunstroke. Women's hairstyles are long and straight. Children have short hair, often with a sidelock on the right-hand side of their heads. A sidelock is a long lock of hair.

WHAT TO EAT

Ancient Egyptian food is very healthy. You'll find fresh fruit, vegetables, and fish on the menu.

The basis of all meals is bread. The ancient Egyptians were the first civilization to use yeast. Yeast makes bread rise. Most people eat a kind of bread made without yeast. This bread is flat. There are also sweet breads. These taste more like cake.

The ancient Egyptians use many herbs and spices in their cooking. If you have a sweet tooth then honey is used instead of sugar.

In this model, bakers are kneading (folding and pressing) dough to make bread.

ROAST PELICAN AND PIGEON

Meat is expensive. The national dish is roasted goose. It is cooked on special occasions. It is eaten by the elite (top people of society). Roast duck, beef, and pigeon are also popular. Pork is not popular. Some people believe that pork carries **leprosy**. Leprosy is a skin disease.

WHAT TO DRINK

The water from the Nile can be dirty. But most local people drink it and survive to tell the tale. Beer is very popular. People often brew it at home. Ancient Egyptian beer is different to today's beer. It is thick, like a milkshake.

The Nile Valley is perfect for growing grapes. These are often used to make wine.

The ancient Egyptians make their own wine. There is also **imported** wine. This means it has come from another country.

MONEY

If you visit during the New Kingdom, you will find that the ancient Egyptians do not use money.

A person's wealth is measured by the number of cattle they own. Ancient Egyptians accept gold and other precious metals for goods and services. They also accept grain and oil.

Pack some things from home that you cannot get in ancient Egypt. These will be excellent for **bartering**. This is when you swap goods rather than using money.

PRICES

The ancient Egyptians price things by using copper weights or rings. These are called debens and seniu.

THE POSTAL SERVICE

Ancient Egyptians use symbols called **hieroglyphs** for writing. **Scribes** will take down your message on **papyrus** (a kind of paper). A scribe is a person who copies messages. Messengers and soldiers carry messages. Messages are also flown by specially trained pigeons!

Grain being harvested by slaves. This could be exchanged for other goods.

PAPERWORK

The ancient Egyptians love their paperwork. Scribes scribble away all day. The ancient Egyptians are very organized. Expect to be delayed on your journey. You will have lots of forms to fill in.

A sailing boat is the best way to travel in ancient Egypt.

CHAPTER 3

TRAVEL, FOOD, AND SHELTER

Most ancient Egyptians live near the Nile. They get about on boats. You can expect to do the same on your visit. When it comes to places to stay, you will be relying on the locals to offer shelter.

If you're lucky you might get a room for the night. Or, you may get a blanket and a place to sleep on the roof under the stars.

TRAVELLING BY BOAT

The best way to travel between places along the Nile is by boat. It is a wonderful experience! Boats travelling southwards use sails. The wind blows the sails. It powers the boats upriver. Boats going north, or downriver, let the river do the work.

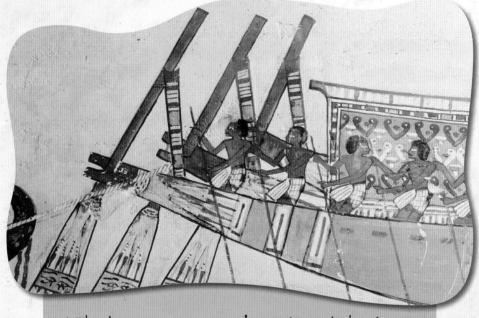

This barge is carrying a **shrine** (sacred place) to a god as part of a funeral ceremony.

The royal family travel in magnificent barges. These have large sails that blow in the wind. There are benches for the oarsmen. If you plan to travel in style then this is the way to go.

RUSH HOUR ON THE NILE

If you have limited money then the ancient Egyptians have excellent river boats. They glide through the water quickly. The river can get busy carrying people and cargo (goods).

TRAVELLING BY LAND

There isn't a network of roads in ancient Egypt. For trips overland farmers and peasants use donkeys and mules. Horses are ridden by the **aristocracy** (nobles).

If you have luggage to carry, visit after 1550 BC. That is over 3,000 years ago. By then the wheeled **chariot** has been invented. A wheeled chariot is a two-wheeled cart.

A **pharaoh** and groom sit on a chariot pulled by a pony.

WHERE TO STAY

In ancient Egypt many people have an open door policy. This means they will invite you to stay in their home.

BUDGET BED AND BREAKFAST

Houses for workers and farmers are usually built of mud bricks. They are built close together. You may be invited to sleep in a small room or even one of the store rooms.

Cooking usually takes place on the roof. If you are lucky there may be a toilet — a hole in the floor. If there are no toilets then there may be a pot. If not, you'll need to find a hidden spot outside!

This model of an ordinary ancient Egyptian house is called a "soul house". It is home for a spirit in the **Afterlife**.

FIVE STAR ACCOMMODATION

You could try to get an invitation to a bigger house. They usually have walled gardens. Inside, there are rooms for entertaining, cooking, and sleeping. There are quarters or living areas for servants and women.

Guests mostly stay on the first floor. The beds are raised from the ground (away from creepy crawlies)!

At the best homes there are bathrooms attached to the bedrooms. Servants give showers by pouring jugfuls of water over you. The toilets are not too bad — a seat on a small platform above a pot.

BOOK A TRIP TO AN OASIS

The more adventurous can travel through the desert to visit an **oasis**. It usually has its own source of water. It takes weeks to reach one. But it is worth it. There is excellent boating, swimming, fishing, and hunting.

The mysterious **Sphinx** watches over the great pyramids at Giza. It has a human head and a lion's body.

CHAPTER 4

WHERE TO GO

There are many wonderful places to visit in ancient Egypt. Most people think about the pyramids first, so a trip to Giza is a must. Some people can't wait to see the magnificent temples at Karnak. It's quite easy to plan a trip that takes in most of the major tourist sites. Most of them are near the Nile. This makes it possible to sail upriver or paddle downriver! Stop off along the way and discover all the treasures.

THE ROYAL CITY OF MEMPHIS

Memphis is an exciting **capital** city on the west bank of the Nile. The city is built on land that used to be flooded by the Nile. Now man-made **dykes** protect it. A dyke is a long wall built to stop flooding.

For an unusual day out visit the bird breeding grounds on the lakes. Birds are hatched and grown here. The ancient Egyptians place **mummified** (see page 17) birds and animals in their tombs. They are there to keep them company in the **Afterlife**.

This tomb is in Saqqara, "the city of the dead".

TOP ATTRACTIONS IN MEMPHIS

- The Palace of Apries: amazing courtyard; throne room with beautiful limestone columns. Columns are tall pillars of stone.
- The Temple of Ptah: you can't see inside but it has a splendid hall with rows of stone columns.
- Fine parks, gardens, and lakes found around the city.

CITY OF THE DEAD

A trip to Saqqara and Giza is the highlight of a visit to ancient Egypt. Saqqara and Giza are known as "the city of the dead", or **necropolis**. There are cemeteries and tombs. There are temples and pyramids. The bodies of the dead **pharaohs** are laid to rest in the pyramids.

THE GREAT PYRAMID

A good time to visit is during the reign of Khufu of the Old Kingdom. He is building the Great Pyramid at Giza.

You will see how the workers haul great chunks of stone across the desert. They do this using wooden rollers. The Great Pyramid is one of the seven wonders of the ancient world.

A TRIP DOWN THE NILE VALLEY

BENI HASAN

It is best to visit the **necropolis** (burial place) Beni Hasan during the Middle Kingdom. The local rulers are building beautiful tombs. Visit the tomb of a local governor called Khnumhotep II. It has some of the most famous art in ancient Egypt.

THE ART OF THE WALL-PAINTER
This wall painting from the tomb of Khnumhotep II shows a slave picking figs.

AKHETATEN

The city of Akhetaten was made for the New Kingdom ruler Amenhotep IV. He started a new religion. It worshipped the Sun god, Aten. As part of the new religion, Amenhotep changed his name to Akhenaten.

Akhetaten has many attractions. For example, the Great Temple of Aten.

The king's wife is called Nefertiti. Rumour has it she is one of the most beautiful women in ancient Egypt. You would be lucky to get a glimpse of her.

ABYDOS

Abydos is a holy place in ancient Egypt. It is the centre of worship to the god of the dead, Osiris. Ancient Egyptians try to visit Abydos once in their lifetime.

Queen Nefertiti and her daughter worshipping the Sun god Aten.

⤴ A magical view across the Sacred Lake of Amun, Karnak.

THEBES

Thebes is the **capital** city of the New Kingdom. On the east bank of the Nile is the trading centre. The temples of Karnak and Luxor are also there. The west bank of the Nile is different. Here is the burial ground for the New Kingdom **pharaohs**. It is called the Valley of the Kings.

THE MAGIC OF KARNAK

You will need a few days to take in all the temples at Karnak. Together they form the largest temple complex in ancient Egypt. There are temples to the gods Amun, Mut, and Khonsu.

The Temple of Amun is reached from the Nile by an avenue of **sphinxes** with rams' heads. A sphinx is a sculpture with a lion's body and a human head. Inside the temple, look out for the **colossus** of Ramesses II. A colossus is a statue which is much bigger than life size.

LUXOR

Luxor Temple is just 2 kilometres (1.2 miles) from Karnak. It is much smaller than Karnak. It has grand attractions. There is a pair of pink granite obelisks. Obelisks are stone pillars with a pyramid-shaped top. They reach 25 metres into the air.

The Sphinxes at Luxor.

INTO THE VALLEY OF THE KINGS

Go to the Valley of the Kings during the early morning or late afternoon. It is cooler then. The dry limestone hills in the Valley of the Kings aren't welcoming. This is why the **pharaohs** chose this place to be buried. They wanted somewhere far away from grave robbers and other people.

The death mask of Tutankhamen. It is buried within his tomb.

The Valley of the Kings is supposed to be a secret place. Plan your trip during the New Kingdom. The tombs are being built then. The tomb of the boy-king Tutankhamen is worth a visit. His mummy is covered with a beautiful golden mask.

One of the two guards outside the entrance to Tutankhamen's burial chambers.

The temple of Queen Hatshepsut in Luxor. She is one of the few female Egyptian pharaohs.

TOP TOMBS

The Valley of the Kings has hundreds of tombs. They have been cut into the cliffs. A few tombs have false burial chambers. They are to trick tomb robbers. Most of the tombs are decorated with wall paintings. These paintings show the journey to the **Afterlife**.

VALLEY OF THE QUEENS

Royal wives and children are buried in the Valley of the Queens. It is rumoured that the most beautiful tomb in all ancient Egypt has been built here. It is for Queen Nefertari.

This colourful wall painting shows the nobleman Nebamun. He is hunting for birds and fish on the Nile.

CHAPTER 5

WHAT TO DO

There's more to ancient Egypt than temples and tombs. Once you've done the sightseeing you might fancy some shopping. Snap up some bargains at the market place. The ancient Egyptians head for the Nile to swim, fish, and hunt. Enjoy the banquets with dancers, acrobats, and musicians. Highlights of the year are the festivals. At the festival of Bastet, all the locals parade in the street.

LET'S SHOP!

The market places of ancient Egypt are filled with a range of food. There are fish, fruit, and vegetables. There are herbs, spices, and home-brewed beer. Visit local craftsmen such as potters, jewellers, and weavers. You can buy handicrafts from them.

The ancient Egyptians have many interesting board games. Some are made in the shapes of animals, like this one.

WHAT TO BUY?

You could buy a typical ancient Egyptian souvenir. You might choose a board game. There are some lovely toys. There are carved ivory animals, dolls, and balls. You could also buy mirrors, fine linen (cloth), and musical instruments.

BEAUTIFUL JEWELLERY

Ancient Egyptian jewellery is very beautiful. People believe that some jewels and gemstones can bring good luck. Lapis lazuli is thought to bring joy and delight. Lapis lazuli is a bright blue gemstone.

Gold is connected to the Sun. Silver is rarer than gold. It is more expensive.

A LASTING MEMORY

Why not ask an artist to paint you on **papyrus** (paper)? Ancient Egyptian artists have their own style. They paint eyes and shoulders as if they were seeing the person from the front. They paint the body side on. See the picture on page 42.

TAKE ME TO THE RIVER

The Nile provides endless ways to have a good time. There is excellent swimming and boating. Boat races and boat games are also popular. Fishing is common. You can hunt birds, crocodile, and hippopotamus.

There is hunting inland too. In the desert people trap animals such as hares, hyenas, and foxes.

Slave girls entertain guests at a banquet with music and dancing.

ENTERTAINMENT

Plays are sometimes performed at the temples. These "plays" are about religion. They are nothing like the theatre you may be used to. People also enjoy watching a kind of ball game. It is similar to hockey.

LAVISH BANQUETS

Ancient Egyptian banquets are a must for any traveller. There is plenty of entertainment. There is music and dancing. There are jugglers and acrobats. Servants will bring you fine food and wine or beer. The ancient Egyptians like to drink a lot of wine and beer.

FESTIVALS

Festivals are an excuse for everyone to enjoy themselves. People eat and drink too much. On the holy day of the cat goddess Bastet, no work is done. People parade in the streets wearing masks.

A nobleman, dressed in a panther skin. He offers lotus and **papyrus** to the god Osiris.

The Eye of Horus often appears on wall paintings. It protects people from evil and ill health.

CHAPTER 6

KEEPING SAFE AND WELL

If you get ill in ancient Eygpt then you'd better believe in magic! People cast spells, or pray to the gods for a cure. They also practise **faith healing**. This uses faith and trust instead of medicine. However, ancient Egypt also has some of the best doctors in the ancient world. There isn't much crime in ancient Egypt. Robbers would rather steal from a tomb than pick your pocket.

HEALTH – WHAT TO EXPECT

Stomach upsets and diarrhoea are common. Most holidaymakers are sick sometime during their visit. It's hardly surprising. People throw human waste outside their homes. Birds, animals, and insects feed on the rubbish. They spread germs. Sunstroke and sunburn can ruin your holiday. Stay in the shade if possible.

DEADLY DISEASES OF ANCIENT EGYPT

- **Cholera**: waterborne disease causing severe diarrhoea and vomiting.
- **Tuberculosis**: airborne disease which affects the lungs.
- **Smallpox**: highly contagious virus; causes spots on the skin which leave scars.
- **Bilharzia**: passed to humans by infected snails living in fresh water.
- **Malaria**: passed to humans by infected mosquitoes.

A VISIT TO THE DOCTOR

Ancient Egyptian doctors are possibly the best you will find in the ancient world. They know a lot about the human body and how it works.

However, the ancient Egyptians haven't quite mastered medicine. They think that the heart is used for thinking. They don't know what the brain is used for. Don't let this worry you. Most doctors use their common sense. They only turn to magic and religion if they can't find a cure.

FIGHTING SICKNESS

Medicine and treatments can be anything from very good to downright odd. It's probably best to avoid cures such as water from pigs' eyes.

Honey is used to kill germs. It helps minor cuts and wounds to heal. Some doctors put raw meat on a bad wound. They say it helps to stop the bleeding.

A doctor treats a patient with an eye problem.

COMMON ANCIENT EGYPTIAN CURES

- **To stop diarrhoea**: take one-eighth of a cup of figs and grapes, bread dough, corn, fresh earth, onion, and elderberry.
- **To cure indigestion**: crush a hog's tooth and put inside four sugar cakes. Eat one cake a day for four days.
- **To ease pain**: anoint the body (cover in oil) and expose to the Sun.

SECURITY

Ancient Egypt is one of the safest places in the ancient world for travellers. People don't use money, so there is little threat from pickpockets. You will travel mostly by boat on the Nile. So you will not need to look out for robbers hiding in the hills. Ancient Egypt is also safe because people have strong religious beliefs (see pages 14–15). Most people try to be honest. That is the best way of making the goddess Ma'at happy.

BEWARE OF THIEVES!

Even though you are quite safe, be on your guard. Thieves may try to steal your luggage. There will always be people who try to take advantage of you.

One of the biggest crimes is tomb robbery. Tomb robbers usually work in teams. They steal from royal tombs. They can take everything from the fine jewellery to the gold fittings on the **sarcophagus** (coffin).

PUNISHMENT

It takes a brave person to rob a royal tomb. The sentence for tomb robbery is death by impalement. This means that the guilty person is lowered on to a sharp stake. He is left to die very slowly.

These men are being led off to be punished for not working hard enough!

The guilty robber is also badly beaten. His body is no use to him in the **Afterlife**. This is a terrible fate for any ancient Egyptian.

For petty crimes people are beaten or whipped. They may have their ears or nose cut off. Ancient Egyptians like their punishments to be painful and quick.

Egyptian **hieroglyphs** (symbols)
are believed to be the first writing
system in the world.

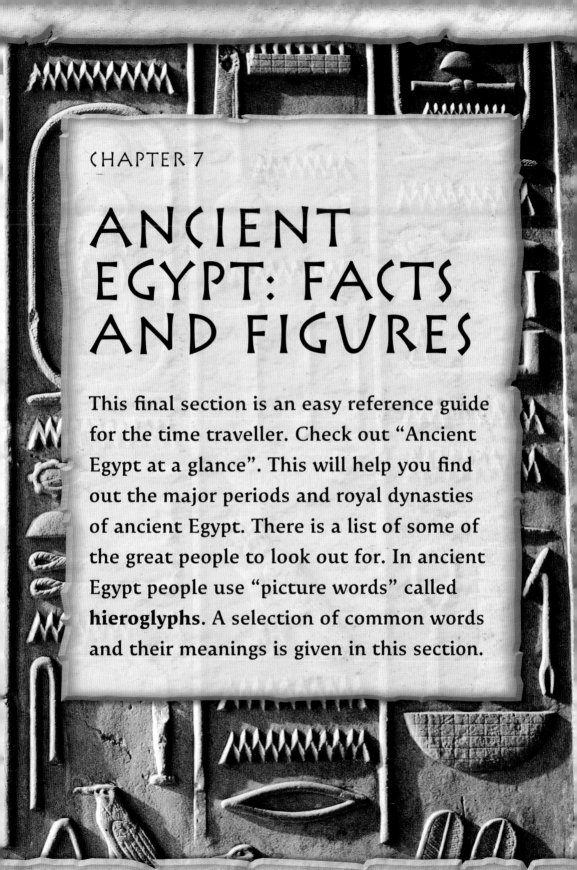

CHAPTER 7

ANCIENT EGYPT: FACTS AND FIGURES

This final section is an easy reference guide for the time traveller. Check out "Ancient Egypt at a glance". This will help you find out the major periods and royal dynasties of ancient Egypt. There is a list of some of the great people to look out for. In ancient Egypt people use "picture words" called **hieroglyphs**. A selection of common words and their meanings is given in this section.

ANCIENT EGYPTIAN PHRASE BOOK

The ancient Egyptians use picture writing called **hieroglyphs**. There are several thousand hieroglyphs. They are beautiful, almost like works of art. The hieroglyphs can be read vertically (up and down) and horizontally (across).

SOME COMMON EGYPTIAN HIEROGLYPHS

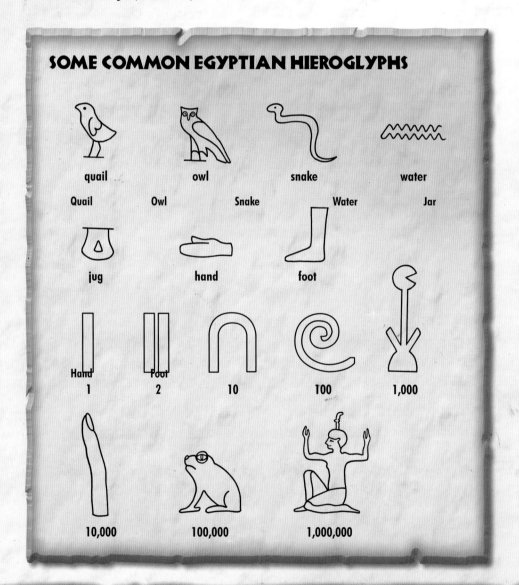

quail	owl	snake	water
Quail	Owl	Snake	Water	Jar

jug	hand	foot

Hand	Foot			
1	2	10	100	1,000

10,000	100,000	1,000,000

USEFUL EGYPTIAN WORDS AND PHRASES

(Pronunciation, or how to say it, is in *italics*)

I = *inek*
my = say *ee* after the word
My name is ... = *ren-ee* ...

Hello = *hee*
Good morning = *sebat neferet*
Good evening = *masheru nefer*

Where (is...)? = *chen...?*
How much (is...)? = *wer...?*
I want, I would like = *mer-ee*

this = *pen*
that = *pef*
there = *im*

water = *mu*
bread = *ta*
figs = *daby*
fish = *rem*
meat = *iwef*
food = *wenemet*
eat = *wenem*
drink = *sewary*

I am/we are hungry = *inek/inu heker*

I am/we are thirsty = *inek/inu ibu*
chariot = *wereret*
to sail south = *henet*
to sail north = *hed*
to sail across = *wedja*
to go = *shem*
Do you go to... = *shem-tenu en*...

bad = *bin*
good = *nefer*
a little (of) = *nehy (en)*

one = *wat*
two = *senu*
ten = *medju*
many = *asha*

today = *hen*
tomorrow = *miseba*
yes = *chew*
no = *nen*

ANCIENT EGYPT AT A GLANCE

TIMELINE
(*Please note that dates are approximate.*)

5500–3000 BC   PRE–DYNASTIC PERIOD
The beginning of hieroglyphic writing

3100–2686 BC   EARLY DYNASTIC PERIOD
The creation of the Egyptian state in about 3250 BC.
3100–2890	1st Dynasty
3100	Narmer (Menes)
2890–2686	2nd Dynasty

2686–2181 BC   OLD KINGDOM
The Great Pyramids at Giza are built.
2686–2613	3rd Dynasty
2686–2667	Sanakht
2667–2648	Djoser
2613–2498	4th Dynasty
2613–2589	Sneferu
2589–2566	Khufu
2558–2532	Khafra
2494–2345	5th Dynasty
2345–2181	6th Dynasty

2181–2055 BC   FIRST INTERMEDIATE PERIOD
Egypt is divided into two states.
2181–2125	7th and 8th Dynasties
2160–2025	9th and 10th Dynasties
2125–2055	11th Dynasty

2055–1650 BC   MIDDLE KINGDOM
*The country is reunited by the **pharaoh** Mentuhotep II.*
2055–1985	11th Dynasty
2055–2004	Mentuhotep II
1985–1795	12th Dynasty
1985–1955	Amenemhat I
1795–1650	13th and 14th Dynasties

1650–1550 BC   SECOND INTERMEDIATE PERIOD

15th, 16th and 17th Dynasties. Dates from this period are not clear. Ancient Egypt is ruled by the **Hyksos** people. Egyptian rulers drive them out. The 17th Dynasty begins.

1550–1069 BC   NEW KINGDOM

Often called the golden age of ancient Egypt. Building work starts at the Valley of the Kings.

1550–1295	18th Dynasty
	Ahmose
1525–1504	Amenhotep I
1473–1458	Queen Hatshepsut
1427–1400	Amenhotep II
1352–1336	Amenhotep IV (Akhenaten)
1336–1327	Tutankhamen
1323–1295	Horemheb
1295–1186	19th Dynasty
1295–1294	Ramesses I
1294–1279	Sety I
1279–1213	Ramesses II
1186–1069	20th Dynasty

1069–747 BC   THIRD INTERMEDIATE PERIOD

Ancient Egypt loses power. It is taken over by Nubian rulers. 21st, 22nd, 23rd, 24th Dynasties rule the country.

747–332 BC   LATE PERIOD

The Assyrians and Persians rule over ancient Egypt. 25th, 26th, 27th, 28th, 29th and 30th Dynasties rule the country.

332–305 BC   THE MACEDONIANS

Alexander the Greek conquers ancient Egypt in 332.

305–30 BC   THE PTOLEMAIC DYNASTY

A troubled time which begins with the rule of Ptolemy I.

51–30	Queen Cleopatra.
30	Egypt becomes part of the Roman Empire.

GREAT ANCIENT EGYPTIANS

- **Imhotep** (around 2675 BC) — designed what was probably the first pyramid — the Step Pyramid at Saqqara.
- **Khufu** (around 2589–2566 BC) — Khufu's kingdom was very strong. His country was never attacked from outside. Khufu is famous for building the Great Pyramid at Giza.
- **Tutankhamen** (died circa 1325 BC) — became **pharaoh** when he was just 9 years old. He died around the age of 18. Some people believe that he was murdered.
- **Ramesses II** (circa 1279–1213 BC) — also known as Ramesses the Great. This mighty pharaoh ruled ancient Egypt for 66 years.

CLEOPATRA: THE LAST RULER OF ANCIENT EGYPT

Cleopatra VII took the throne aged 19. She shared it with her brother, Ptolemy XIII. Ptolemy forced Cleopatra into exile (sent away from Egypt). She joined forces with a Roman general called Julius Caesar. Caesar drove Ptolemy out. Cleopatra regained her throne. Cleopatra gave birth to Caesar's son, Caesarion. Caesar was killed in 44 BC. That was over 2,000 years ago. Cleopatra ruled Egypt with her son.

Cleopatra then had a relationship with the Roman leader Mark Antony. The Roman Empire started war against Egypt. Cleopatra is said to have killed herself by getting an asp (snake) to bite her. She was the last ruler of ancient Egypt.

FURTHER READING

BOOKS

Amazing Facts about Ancient Egypt, James Putnam and Jeremy Pemberton (Thames and Hudson, 1994)

Ancient Egypt: Eyewitness Guide, George Hart (Dorling Kindersley, 2002)

The Awesome Egyptians (Horrible History series), Terry Deary and Martin Brown (Scholastic, 1993)

Encyclopedia of Ancient Egypt (Usborne Publishing Ltd, 2004)

Hieroglyph Handbook: Teach Yourself Ancient Egyptian, Philip Ardagh (Faber and Faber, 1999)

WEBSITES

- http://www.guardians.net/egypt/kids
An excellent list of links to children-friendly sites.

- http://www.ancientegypt.co.uk/menu.html
The website for the British Museum.

- http://www.nationalgeographic.com/media/tv/mumquiz/mummyquiz1.html
A quick quiz to find out just how much you know about how to make a mummy.

GLOSSARY

Afterlife place where ancient Egyptians believed the dead went

amulet good luck charm, often worn as jewellery

aristocracy highest social rank in society, the nobility

barter to trade by exchanging food or other goods rather than using money

capital most important city in a country. It is usually the centre of government.

chariot small, two-wheeled cart that is pulled by a horse or mule

colossus statue which is much bigger than life size

delta area where a river begins to spread out into several channels before it reaches the sea

dyke long wall or embankment which is built to stop flooding, especially from rivers or the sea

empire group of countries or lands that are controlled by one ruler

faith healing way of healing a person using faith and trust, often in religion, rather than medicine

fertile something that is rich and full of goodness. Fertile land is good for growing plants and crops.

hieroglyphs symbols and pictures that are used in ancient Egyptian writing

Hyksos group of foreign people, probably from Palestine or Syria

import to bring foreign goods into another country

leprosy skin disease which can cause parts of skin and limbs to rot away

mummification the process of preserving a dead body and wrapping it in bandages

mummified when a dead body is specially preserved

necropolis ancient cemetery or burial place

oasis fertile area in the desert with its own natural source of water

papyrus reed that the ancient Egyptians made into paper

pharaoh ancient Egyptian king

plague deadly disease which spreads quickly over a wide area

sarcophagus stone coffin which is often decorated with sculptures or carved inscriptions

scribe person whose job it is to copy books or documents by hand

shrine place that is sacred to a god or holy person

silt fertile mud washed up from the riverbed during floods

sphinx stone sculpture with a lion's body and a human head

vizier chief advisor to the pharaoh

INDEX